TRANSITION VAMPS

DAVID PRATER

Other publications by David Prater

POETRY

Leaves of Glass

Morgenland

We Will Disappear

DAVID PRATER

TRANSITION VAMPS

CORDITE BOOKS 06 06

First printed in 2026
by Cordite Publishing Inc.
PO Box 58
Castlemaine 3450
Victoria, Australia
cordite.org.au | corditebooks.org.au

National Library of Australia
Cataloguing-in-Publication:

Prater, David
Transition Vamps
978-0-6457616-9-6 paperback
I. Title.
A821.3

Poetry set in Lora 10 / 15
Cover design by Zoë Sadokierski
Text design by Kent MacCarter and Zoë Sadokierski
Printed and bound by McPhersons in Maryborough, Victoria

10 9 8 7 6 5 4 3 2 1

For Kathleen

CONTENTS

PREFACE

It's hardly controversial to claim that daily life contains transitions. From sleep to wakefulness, REM states to proto-circadian lucidity, pre- to post-caffeine, horizontal to vertical, a.m. to p.m., light to darkness. But many of the day's transitions also repeat, like a jazz combo vamping while the lead sax or guitar shapes beauty out of curved air. Infinite *pomodoro* cycles of existence, timeboxes crammed with discrete thoughts, zen's meditative end-games.

One Swedish word for transition is 'övergång', a word I love for the ö with its umlaut, the å its overring. My first experience of the endless daylight of the northern hemisphere summer left me delirious, awake half the 'night', drifting in and out of sleep during 'daylight' hours. The sensation of sleeping and dreaming in sunlight was strange: it upended my day's diurnal rhythm. I often woke feeling as if I'd just entered a new dimension.

While not every poem in this collection was written in Sweden, or concerns transitions, I wanted it to express how feeling strange and alienated became a kind of home for me, especially there. I wanted to fill it with songs of transit, elegies to disappeared stars and soundtracks to chaos in the physical and imaginary worlds. To admit the furious unpredictability of life, and of love's languages. To re-arrive, breathless and confused, in a place I've never visited.

The word 'övergång' has other potential meanings. The 'över' can just mean over, but also of, above, on, across, past, throughout or via. A 'gång' might refer to time, the act of walking, a transfer, a corridor or aisle, running, working, a pathway, a passageway or the treading of feet. Re-combining any two of these definitions implies the possibilities of all the others. I hope *Transition Vamps* acts as a transfer ticket for you, or someone like you, walking past.

INTRODUCTION

David Prater's singular punctuation mark is the parenthesis which Renaissance humanist and theologian Erasmus, an early booster of that particular glyph, dubbed *lunulae*; translation: little moons. It is a perfectly Praterian coinage that encapsulates the waxing and waning halves intended to quarantine asides or afterthoughts. But in Prater's work, more often than not, the waning bracket appears without its waxing reflection, fostering ambiguity and opening up a poem's possibilities, particularly when used in rapid succession:

> The first email (never sent
> CCed Gaia but bounced. So *it goes* ... (that manual exchange
> inside a Powerhouse (a museum exhibit etched in charcoal
> rides the lightning (killing composers, developing in still-life. ('Wireless')

It is worth considering where the first missing bracket would be placed if punctuation were being used conventionally. Probably after 'sent', though the information it would contain is hardly an afterthought, indeed it transforms the meaning of the second part of the sentence. The ambiguity expands with the second missing bracket. Should it be deployed after Powerhouse or is the third (even the fourth?) opening bracket nested inside the second? These questions expand exponentially through the poem, turning into a kind of magic box, a steampunk automaton that, once a mechanism is triggered, takes on a life of its own, all spinning cogs and whirring gears. The possibilities the open brackets create propel the poem towards, as Baudelaire put it, '*l'expansion des chose infinies.*'

The unbounded expansion of possibilities, of language, poetics and meaning, gives the poems in *Transition Vamps* their momentum. It is a peripatetic collection with poems set variously in Korea, Sweden, the Netherlands and Australia. The poet is a foreigner aslant his world. But it also shows up in less predictable ways.

For instance internet poems, including '(On the tomb of) Ephrem Tamiru', 'and 'Victor Garber Blooper Reel', both of which chart journeys through YouTube comments on videos about, respectively, an Ethiopian pop star and a lead actor in the spy show *Alias*, tumble down a social media rabbit hole, the kind of nodal knowledge journey the internet has acculturated us to. The poems move with the stutter step of a mouse's scroll wheel and the teleportation of a clicked link.

In 'Kus', a discursive poem à la mid-career John Ashbery, the searching is the desire to 'really learn' the Dutch language's 'beautiful word for a kiss'. We should, the poem argues, be able to know these words that are 'not meant/ to live in a dictionary but in/the mouth'. There seems to be a yearning for this knowledge to be a kind of fixed tangible state, a game show prize you can hold in your hands.

Instead, language is 'like a shiny/spaceship forever tumbling towards/ the *kus*.' The line break is telling. Prater's poetry is often tumbling towards something, in this case the kus, but, just as often, it is just tumbling towards. Maybe the best we can hope for is what Wendy James sang about: 'I don't want your car baby/ I want your ah!'

—Liam Ferney

Övergången

This is the phase you will need to get through
        quickly now. It's already too late to plead
ignorance, or a special case. You've strayed in-
        to the grey zone between care factors. On one
hand: zero. And on the other: none. Someone
        is about to tap you on the shoulder, asking for
something: papers, identity, drugs. It doesn't
        matter what they want, exactly; only how you
react. It must be in time. It must seem casual,
        beyond effortless. You must act as if you truly
could not care less. This is good. This is very,
        very good. As a reward, please find two single
bus tickets enclosed. The first one will get you
        to the station. The second has already expired.

come with me, through

the gate, we'll find the way
but hurry, do, okay? The path is
hidden but there all the same—
the leaves will disguise it again
when we've passed. Follow the
children, they'll know the way;
somehow their feet always find
the smoothest stones. Run with me.
This way is safer & farther away
from the noise, from what chases us.
It's always there, so start running.

Your belly is not yet a bomb.
Your belly does not hide a bomb.

You fly up & over the gate.
You brush the last leaves on the
bough & they fall off, disguising
our path. There is a child running
ahead of us. She appears to know
the way ahead but hesitates & turns
to look at me. Do you know the
way? she asks, & you bundle
her up in your skirts & we run.

Your belly is not a bomb.
Your belly does not hide a bomb.

Anti-kraak

in the new *anti-kraak* universe you play *squatter*
upside-down in your brain at parties you proffer

slim handshakes, some modest attempts at *Dutch*
& a determination to stand there all day like a *boer*

in a landscape where he is *Indigenous* – the *white*
light shining from his invisibly big head; yet you

fall under the dim star of sleep (where eerie *canals*
watch you breathe & you *stagger* from one station

to another – drugged by *sundown*, watching the big
orange heat ball swinging *royally* low over the *meer*

a cardboard world where *settlers* merrily *invade* each
other after dinner ... you lose a *continent* over coffee

or else blood-red *wijn*, a casualty of summer time
where the day & the air & the land *are belong* to us

clouds, afternoon, jazz, sprinkles

for Jill Jones

1. clouds

Abercrombie Street, Chippendale

Reading your electrical poems in a Northcote bar
in winter was too much: like trying to drink
beer sailing freely through the air: free of the glass,
sure, but harder than buckshot to catch between
teeth. I longed for some of that Sydney where
July was windy and wet but not cold. I wanted
to perch in that laundromat on Abercrombie Street
just down from the Reasonably Good Café, chew
on an Incredibly All Right Ham Sandwich™, read
William Faulkner's *Light in August* (i-in August!
& simply wait for September's frangipani booms
to ricochet down the Chippendale lanes like odd
socks above Central Station or perhaps (sure, in
desperation, to close my eyes & also disappear.

2. afternoon

Foveaux Street, Surry Hills

I could pretend to live somewhere else, I guess
but all I can think about now is how clichéd
Sydney must have been in the 1920s, the Futurism
of Bondi travel posters aside (undergrad hat tip!
I'd already been there, once, maybe. With a girl.
I wish I could turn to poetry the dismally banal
warehouse districts (c. bottom end of Foveaux St.
& surrounds, Ctrl+Alt+Del every whipped
palm tree by the Elizabeth St. entrance to Central,
blow up the blackboard menus outside the faux
cafes 'adorning' streets where journos used to
drink the afternoon away, like the one where we
caught up, once, in a previous carnation. Yeah,
everything was chic & *Quadrant* didn't even exist.

3. jazz

Oceanic Café, Elizabeth Street

A little bird inside my cranium orders me to write
a poem on the subject of the Oceanic Café which
once peddled its wares on Elizabeth Street but
I can't do it. Who would care? All it ever seemed
to serve was steak and peas & I never ventured
inside there anyway. Too busy moping, probably.
Why? They removed the soul of Strawberry Hills
just to make houses from its yellow clay years ago
& the pub that shares its name has since stopped
playing its bad jazz. Oh yes, blows away the melody
it does, just like a wind chime. Cue ragged Tibetan
prayer flags. The paper carries yet another article
about the Australian poetry, written for the over-
68s. Cue Transvision Vamp, baby. 'I don't care.'

4. sprinkles

Grace Bros, Broadway

I'm reminded of sprinkles, the way they insinuate
loss, or themselves. That's insider culture! & how
we insulate ourselves from change (unless it's the
climate at stake – in which case Sydney blows bum
notes all along 'Broadway'. What's left? Do I light
another Craven A? Crack a silver bullet? A clove?
Chomp down on the deadly sausages Bert Newton
ate in *Fatty Finn*? Gawd, I miss Noni Hazelhurst!
Pardon me while I dream of the days when trams
lit up Sydney's skies with meteor showers (or were
they sparks? Think I might take another spacewalk,
this time in the direction of Central Station, pop in to
Our Lady of Snows. Free meals, clouds. Afternoons.
Jazz. Everywhere you look: Hundreds & Thousands.

Imjingang sax scene

for Ivy Alvarez

the appositeness of the phrase *getting off at redfern*
struck our roving correspondent with all the force of
teutonic bombs as the limousine bus pulled into that
wind-blasted car-park near the old Imjingang station

last stop before a river crossing (over a broken bridge
the one that used to go to *Chosŏn*, the other mystical
fatherland (that got waylaid by *Arirang* & *Sŏn'gun*,
that number one hit with a bullet known as *Chuch'e*

picture then the scene complete with invisible sax
as tourists wandered around wrecked locomotives,
strolling nonchalantly beside ponds filled with lilies
& over everything piped or were they real sax sounds

appearing out of nowhere or else an ancestor park –
the sax player herself

oh ajumma

oh broken world

Terminal 2: Air France

> 'Ayant l'expansion des choses infinies'
> —Charles Baudelaire, 'Correspondances'

They transport us in pneumatic tubes, although the pillars
bear traces of correspondence between underlined words;
men and women stop, each becoming an abstract symbol
noticing a tourist poster, finding pat-down rituals familiar.

These queues designed purely and inevitably to confuse us
single file, in huddles, familial groups: we display our unity,
concourses hinted at behind clouds, the capital-city clarity,
know, as we do, the ritual's melody and do not correspond.

Speak slowly, explain it patiently, as a father to children,
morning breaths a mere memory now, like foggy meadows,
watching us pass through the shining gates, triumphant.

Holding back the power to delay or intervene in the infinite,
a searchlight trained on an old dam's wall. And the incense,
who thought of that? A final salute to the terminal of senses.

Hoju/Hanguk (Slight Return)

Then I realised I was halfway through my journey
        waiting for a phone call (but I couldn't remember

my own name (waking up to the sound of a drill
        wearing a t-shirt backwards I heard the dogs bark

outside (artists drank soju & looked at leaves as if
        they were maps & the traffic was silent & to meet

travellers who might be gone by nightfall, oh! wash-
        ing piling up in my room without detergency when

I didn't need a candle without a breeze from the sea
        & showering under a cold hose (passing an *ajumma*

out the front of her seafood restaurant (grabbing my
        arm and smiling, like the girls holding hands at the

markets (green revenue stamps from the immigration
        department layered like a thinking plate of kim chi

& of my faraway family (or an overwhelming grief
        humid as bowls of bubbling soup (then a phone call

made it all different (where old men sit in the park
        on newspapers listening to trills of ladies, raccoon

dogs, sweet stalls (in season now or on the verge of
        turning (my wallet bulges in my pocket, staring at

holes in the base camp of empty soju glasses, watching
        Koreans dreaming on the subways or standing in lines

(catching pigeons with a net, eating alone in a city
        where people eat together, pore over Hangul scripts

crossing roads & counting seconds as lights change
        checking emails with a wasted mosquito and a ceiling

fan buzzing in my ears, fishing for hope in streams & step-
        ping over puddles of spittle in the street (I no longer

remember Australian radio (those were the days – now
        I drink coffee from cans in the land of caffeine calm

(Occulus) Rifts

—Oneohtrix Point Never

I see a universe when he opens his little-boy mouth:
the craggy moon mountains of his pale jagged teeth
watch his eyes tilting back to look at faraway things

I see myself as some kind of mystic Geppetto (busy
lengthening and adjusting my songs and swan strings
& when the rift appears his body relaxes into mine

he is a starship, *Narcissus*, invincible in a flying mask
cruising crazy flight paths guided by algae rhythms
I am a puppet preacher at some river-space baptism

drop into my arms as you did when you were one
minute old) I will hold you in the control room's glow
prepare snacks for us & then boot up the consoles

welcome to your world for I am merely living in it
I bring you down gently onto some small round dais
while an eye and a mountain and a moon look on

Folding their clothes

> 'A daddy who is sleeping can't come running to take care of things.
> And if no one comes when you call, you might as well be quiet.'
>
> —Gunilla Bergström, *God natt, Alfons Åberg*

they will just move on once we are gone, of course;
what choice do they have, after all? perhaps none –

their play-filled days a soundscape we cannot hear,
we can't pretend to know if they'll sleep or eat enough

to get them through it; but should they fall asleep
in a park somewhere, who will be there to hold them?

surely that new friend, the one they met here once,
will come along with smiles and new ideas for games?

(we must rely on this idea of new friends with games,
otherwise there's nothing to hold onto in the dark,

say, when we listen for some sniff or cough and realise
their nightmares were really our own (oh! but look –

the moon falls behind a tree and we say: 'goodbye!'
just fold their clothes, then try extra hard not to cry

drift: a way

'Kraftledningarna/spända i köldens rike/norr om all musik.'
—Tomas Tranströmer

1.

Attention! You are not dreaming, you are drifting
    into sleep. You are feeling veeerrry sleepy now.

The curvature of the earth is causing you to shift
    away from the point that you circled yesterday

on a map, your eyes hazed. That was also a today,
    in a novel fashion – the today of days gone by,

of clouds transformed into rain, or else snow
    drifts. That's okay, you know this: in cathedrals

of bone we find arcs that promise warmth. In drift-
    wood we find the puzzles that madden us all

night, Tetris dreaming. In from our past, deriving
    steam, straight lines, axes, branches, kindling.

2.

Attention! Does anyone here speak Spanish? *Si?*
Bueno! Dream with me. Cry out and into your sleep.

Step fearfully onto the ice and drift a while,
inside a massive Perspex speech-bubble dream.

A white orb longing to become detergent, or aliens, or
Spain. The louvres of a ribcage snapping shut. Awe.

Curvature of the earth is a con job: ask a dervish.
Hail an imaginary cab on a hail-struck avenue

and wait for the popcorn to drop. Stop, drifter!
In the pharmacies and in the alleys, popping

rocks while money men drift by in reddish stockings,
purling and unfurling their ways, their means.

3.

Attention, people! Abstraction hurts. Reading
    too much into things I know nothing about,

the niceness of the void or else a philosopher's
    mouth sewn shut. I know about that, at least:

the madness of seeking asylum in Antipodean
    dreams, drifting for weeks at a time on a boat

more abstract than surreal. Oh, fuck *Life of Pi*!
    Heaven basks like a warm, square meal but

I can't get there from here. There is no shark
    travelling at speed X while I zoom at speed

Y in the opposite direction. I can't use a lasso.
    I no longer have fits, a Vespa. I'm mad. Too bad.

4.

Attention! Ambient doom hunters! Over!
        The curvature of a yawn, a dream sewn shut.

This skin that knows my dreams forgets me.
        Fruit Tingles, wet on the tongue: get me some

analogue hits, expressways to frozen, lakeside
        moon-dream voiceovers. The narrator's cues

infuse the afternoon, the canoes, with nostalgia.
        Somewhere, out *there*, we become driftories.

We lie down in atoms and the clinamina bore.
        We fight against our own handwritten lies,

type marching letters into files and save. Awe.
        Fidelity is a kind of surveillance. Current A.

5.

Attention! It was never my intention to score
    cheap points at the expense of polar bears,

of driftwood, shores. The cockatoos roar. Their
    explosive chatter could strip a conifer raw.

Implant in me some destructive grace, to drift, pine.
    Planetoid lamps all along the turnpike's busy

arcs. Extreme emissions of things. Drift-rings.
    The target of my gaze, sewn shut. Your eyes

rising slower than a star from what you read,
    condensed into steam, here, *north of all music.*

Driftories, signal fires, smoke: disappear. Go
    back to sleep now. No, we were never here.

new space seasons

1. *high*

season before anyone gets there. clean airports. season for new roads and sidewalks. haircuts to die for. fancy dress outfitters. convenience stores. spare parts for rocket ships. strong coffee.

2. *slack*

season of our eventual reunion. in a sunny room where it's always possible to forecast the weather. bicycle riding. small kittens and dictionaries. rocks thrown at windows. expensive bath mats. blindfolds. champagne.

3. *wet*

season of immigration towers and state peace. Aladdin released. addresses blocked. visas refused. unfinished books. boredom. looping playlists. correspondences. hot telephones. text. scarves. puddles throwing a 404.

4. *slow*

season of skyline highs. arranging escapes. tossing out old clothes. empty flats. one bowl of milk per day. subtitles and dangerous sunglasses. blurry stars. postcards. batteries. brocoli. delicious.

København Trilogy

I

‘Morten, who was *not so good to English*,
wore oversized glasses that made his face
look crooked, as if he had been punched,
on a train, by some thug from Århus. We
corresponded only briefly, when we
were both in primary school, but yesterday
I felt his presence in the capital, København,
like a scab slowly peeling itself off my face.
The things he liked to do, his hobbies and
favourite sports, elude me, although football
must be in there somewhere. I am left with
a simple image: a boy carrying a backpack
and wearing a black beanie, travelling alone
on a train in the so-called happiest country
in the world, watching as fields of grey metal
glide by in complete silence. Maybe I should
blame Peter Høeg for putting the image there.
I mean, who else? I want to write him a letter,
ask him if Morten drew a slash through his Os,
the way I used to cross my Ts, dot my Is.’

II

'We'll imagine that for Morten, at his age anyway,
the idea of a girlfriend was preposterous. School
being the great equaliser, we'll creepily approve of
the idea that he was bashed, daily. His parents,
having also been victims of working-class hate,
were powerless to stop it, despite their letters
to the schools department, the weekly protests.
You can guess why Morten's on the train, then:
he's running away to København, or else further,
across the Øresund Bridge, to Malmö. Let's allow
him to get that far, perhaps further still, before
the Polisen corner him in Lund, their windbreakers
catching him in a patriarchal embrace, knocking
his glasses from his face, spilling the contents
of his backpack across the icy platform for anyone
to see. No papers, barcode – no true identity
to speak of. It's a long way from Århus to Lund
but his father drives virtually non-stop through
a horizontal blizzard, pausing once to pay a toll
on the Øresund Bridge, and a second time to cry.'

III

‘I only ran away that one time, fleeing violence
the way refugees flee internment camps, or else
momentary ceasefires. They amount to the same
thing: entering that gap in space between days,
running fast like my old football coach taught me,
head down, fists like pistons. I thought my black
tracksuit would camouflage me against the night,
the mean streets of Nørrebro. As it turned out,
in København I couldn't even leave the station,
surrounded by Tivoli's dregs and angel's wings.
I rode black on a train bound for Malmö instead,
got as far as Lund before the future caught up
with me. I waited for my father in a juvenile cell
crowded with boys who jeered, then broke my
glasses. I only managed to get one solid punch in
before being king-hit from behind, but it was
worth it. Then, on the long drive back to Jylland,
for some reason I recalled that Australian boy
who pretended to be my penpal for a month or
two, in primary school. *Hvad var hans navn?*'

You have memories

You have memories, sure, but then who doesn't
know where you live these days? Camping out in
the foothills until the controversy blew over
seemed like a good idea at the time, of course,
but that was before the anaesthetics kicked in
and you lay there, boiling, and unable to feel
the sweat rolling down your leg. They hacked it
off with a kind of efficiency that was easy to
mistake for care but who's complaining now? Not
you! Because you've still got your wits, and the
planes don't fly so low anymore, and you never
were a big fan of running anyway. Yeah, memories,
how about them! Now you get to control when
they appear, for example, or when to delay them,
send them bawling into your dreams with a swish,
the warlords gesturing over 3D maps of mosques,
glistening rivers barely visible between the cracks
of glaciers sliding across deadened moonscapes,
ordnance going off, adrenalin bangs in capsule
form, and still you bray: Bring it on, Charlie!
like you mean it, like you'd never really forgotten
where you hid them, typing in your new password
without even looking, or deliberately keying in
gibberish answers to standard security prompts.
Name of first pet? Eklhferlhl. First girlfriend?
Gpwjfrqe;ngqgnqgwgq Nhwerppqqhpi. That
should keep them busy for a day or two, at least –
just like in that episode of *Designated MacGyver*.

dress young

you dress young but then you doubt it –
(take a look at the band & think who
are these idiots? remember to dress
young & feel slightly allergic to the
music while all around you (idiots!
fawn over this old band, that New Order
remember the way you dressed when
you were younger (although not quite
as young as your sister was the night
you accompanied her to Bikini Kill at
the Wollongong Youth Centre (or would
'chaperoned' be a better word? hmmm,
you remember Kathleen Hanna shoving
an old-school telephone down the front
of her undies (remember what it felt
like to feel old? as the cool blasts of
chill-wave air smacked your face head-
on ... you were too old to remember
the proton energy pills but *Nevermind*
I mean, forget it (I saw the future in

a room full of moshing girls the minor
threat of sk8rs hanging outside (bored
boys who told stories about sk8n 'n'
shit (did they also dress young? you
betcha (of all people! you grow old,
you shall trade in that dud album by Bob
Mould for a second-hand copy
of *Theatre of Gnomes* nobody knows
the 'Shakedown' finale better than us!
me (I've seen spew coming out of a Port
Kembla sky, it's just steam, some idiot
once claimed (*yeah* & there's nothing
polluting about it ... you grow old
but continue to dress young like some
fifty-year-old drunk wearing *Okanuis*
extra-bitter still got it but forever
yearning for that Clayton's moment
(whatever *that* was – aww, *Nevermind*
dress young (grow old & die

(smiling

Terminal 1: Aer Lingus

> 'A dictionary of shelter'
> —John Tranter, 'Lufthansa'

Flying over Violet-Crumble seas, eyes bulging as the rock
rushes by (a sense of stained-glass futures, a fatal diorama
I'm descending through time with an airman's precision –
the shroud of a cloud's lop-sided laptop strata slips a little
as I glimpse the patchwork, or a field, or a metaphor (and
bank (becoming faintly religious – see the world's correction
while my references slide: taking apart the allusion of mist
with the probability of coffee (or, at least, 'creamer' – o-or
you declare that *the card does not want to be tapped* (smile
as you have been trained, brave crew! Your make-up that is
almost too thick, applied elsewhere: in Ennis for example,
a good time always to be had up there (yr unknown hands
of analogue, orange nail-polish, perfectly parsing the lines
to a post-landing *denouement*, all yr Gaelic letters spelling
HUMANISM, or was it the pilot, nailing his 180 like a motto
whispered to the Shannon runway? Leaning to the far side

(– aww, my nearest exit *was* behind me!

of the sky, an absentee landlord in hot pursuit. That the sun
has a lens flare, or some deliberate, obscured designer's flaw
is not worth contemplating at this height. It's your old flame.
And there to meet you by the car-hire desk, her hair: grey
shakes in your wake (wait – never mind, can you navigate it?
The car-hire parking area's squashed cigarette-butt promises
speak their way into the vehicle, while you punch its screen,
its prior agreements about alcohol-free beers (stumble back
to a crowded cafe, somewhere, perchance to dream a drink
trolley, the zeitgeist clinging to all the beards like raindrops,
a smudge of toothpaste in your reflection, in every porthole
blitzes of twisted shandy (wake: order a no-name lemonade
and note that your ancestors grew no taller than this ceiling.
No, there's mime in the genealogy centre, or was it Katharina
sleeping on the tight ship whose mistress she is, sir? Captain
lifts a hiking trail brieflet from a plastic display case on a wall
explaining Dysert O'Dea Castle & Environs as if 'twere a lake
as (no time for maudlin, no maiden – you send it elsewhere
under bridges where a river moves fast (& floating in it, stars.

(On the tomb of) Ephrem Tamiru

Ephrem Tamiru! tell us what you think re:
        Anchin Kalmeselesh or else just the sax
(slow and shark-like snarling through
        an Asmara bar to hit Thomas Keneally
cold in the nose like a sweet tea might
        were it to care for snark or saxophone
dreams thoughtful as Hammond organ
        licks kicking the Amharic dawn (was it
Amharic, Ephrem? why did they call
        your 1982 cassette-tape album *Shegeye*?
I feel kind of bad for the blogophiles
        downloading yr trax frantically to get
the info (titles translations set-lists etc.
        Ephrem's sound worlds unfurling slow
as Stevie Wonder's imagination (you
        were Ethiopia's Stevie, always will be
mine what does it mean Atawquatim
        the drums tell me what it all means
can't go back to my indie daze now
        I've got Ephrem in the mound of love
in the mouth a super-Saharan man
        pre-beat jazz combo smoking suits
preserved in shellac YouTube amber
        I want to die in the arms of my lover
while she plays the sax on 'Track Six'
        whatever it's called) I guess you don't
accept PayPal, Ephrem, but I want to
        breathe in all of your transmissions
putting Amhara back on the stage –
        blast Ephrem Tamiru onto the page

A movie set in the Middle East

Somewhere, someone's filming a movie set in the Middle East. It's not the Middle East, but we're led to believe we're there, in a crowded marketplace, waiting for something to happen. Does that scare you? It's supposed to. Does it frighten you, too? The way documentaries do? A criminal mastermind sits in a barbershop, being shaved. This scares me. An underling brings bad news. The mastermind waves the barber away, pulls off the white smock, the shaving cream still smeared all over his face, his face half-shaved. I'm scared of that, too. I no longer frequent markets. I stay home at night, the curtains drawn. It's like I'm dreaming, or underwater but I'm scared, that's all. I'm scared of men. This world. Their bright lies dressed as ideas. The rain that makes night. The train that doesn't stop. That scares me, still. The questions we refuse to ask. The dreams we refuse to remember. The planes I refused to see streaking across the desert sky. The taxes I ignored as shopping lists slammed into hillsides. Does it scare you? I'm scared of the things we pretend we don't do. I'm stuck in a movie set in the Middle East. Something's about to happen, but I don't yet know who to. I look around, and all I see is fear. When the blast comes I'm scared I'll miss it. I always miss it. People call me scary. But maybe they're scared of me, too.

'Т'га за југ'

let's pretend I'm an eagle: okay, now, here are my wings,
and with them I shall launch myself from this obscure eyrie,
and together with my fellows!

[yea, comrade eagles!]

I will fly back to my own beaches, my own daylight savings time,
to see the surf club at Ballina, to witness the sunset at Yamba,
and then to sleep on the beach all night so as to catch
the sunrise. W00Ot! and to ask myself,
knowing the answer: could Brunswick Heads ever be as miserable
as old Europe sometimes is (that is, on the days when it rains?

[which means most days! LOL!]

and then, if the rhetorical answer is no, then it's all settled:
I'll sit and watch that sun rising until it burns my scalp,
until its death rays meet my bald crown in a victorious union,
and I'll slip on a shirt, slop on sunscreen and slap on a hat;
yes, even though I'm an eagle and have no need of such things,
I'll pack them into a small dilly bag and attach it to my claw
right before I launch myself from my faraway eyrie and—

[*hang on, didn't I just—*
ehm ...]

oh, I shall replay my grand ascent from my eyrie just for kicks.
and then wait for myself on the briny shore of Lake Ainsworth,
near Lennox Head there,
where Kombie-van campers wear petunia-coloured Crocs,
and the skirts of young women have been sewn with stars.

and why shall I re-do all of these things I have already done?
why, to remind myself of the fact that here, in the cold north,
I am surrounded by a cold, clammy dark that knows my name,
a dark fog disguising itself as some kind of cool suede jacket;
yea, because here the winter lasts for six months of the year,
and the sea freezes itself and pops, then disappears,
the snow blows horizontally, and is generally a big nuisance.
snow everywhere, in cupboards, soccer balls and underwear –
and inside my breasts reside many ice-cold and evil thoughts ...

[*right, so you're now a female eagle and—*]

[**SHUT UP**]

and so this is why I cannot possibly stay here a moment longer –
no, not even for a nano-second, with snow inside my underpants.
let me pretend that I'm an eagle, as in this poem's first line,
and let me simply, rhetorically and magnificently don my wings

[as though I need to actually put them on]

and fly non-stop, or perhaps with a brief stopover in Singapore –
or maybe even Bangkok – no, make it Singapore, okay? as I said,
non-stop to Coolangatta International Airport, where a shuttle
bus shall await me, and I travel on it, onwards to Stradbroke,
or maybe just settle in a heap in Byron Bay. there dwell tourists
who shall tend to my tired wings, who like to twirl fire sticks
after dark on the beach, and who are generous with the makings
when rolling those peculiar patchouli cigarettes of theirs ...

yes, and after the sun has gone down totally, and I look up to
the wooded hillsides dotted with million-dollar bungalows, i'll
see the intense wisdom on nature's part in beckoning me here,
where pizza crusts and empty chip packets proliferate in carparks
and I can stuff myself silly on unsophisticated carbohydrates.

[zzzzzzzzzzzzzzzz ...]

then, and only then, i'll rise once more (sure, a little clumsily)
from my doona, Paddle-Pop-stick and Hypercolour-t-shirt eyrie,
and fly a few clicks south to the shore of Lake Ainsworth, right by
the old Department of Sport and Recreation camp there, and I'll
just park myself for a millennium or so, and watch the ti-tree
waters rippling in the breeze, or in the wake of some kid playing
hide and seek with the sky. after all, beauty is beautiful where-
ever you look for or find it. so let me perch, undisturbed, in
the branch of an otherwise unremarkable tree, preferably green;
let the sun set slowly over the whole tableau like the light at
the end of a movie, and let me die there, one day,

cradling my children in my arms.

Simply Wizard

—Enid Blyton

sounds of our dormy lights-out voices
spilling terrified tales in the eaves

hair-raising feats of a *bulle* named Barry
creep softly over our beds of leaves

perfectly fine to fall asleep mid-sentence
extend your arms (or simply breathe

the sun trail led us home of a morning
back to our breakfast-table futures

fill a *mand* with non-matching mittens
winter heeft geen tijd for moochers

peek through crinkly patchwork panes
stray flakes from a story blizzard

nestling down in the *bedstee* for days
(– everything's just *simply wizard*

Sunshine for Kim Dae-jung

on the day you died I heard helicopters
& jet planes flying over Seoul's old head
the sun was shining heat & burning down
Teheran-ro & the steel streets of Gangnam
were full of girls holding fabric umbrellas
by the subway entrance a young man held
the hands of an older man who was writing
something on a small pad, both looking sad
I don't know why, though I knew it wasn't
you; & as I walked down the stairs into the
subway station I watched girls coming up
holding handbags over their behinds to
prevent the up-skirt glances & cameras
i'd recently read were on the increase ...

i knew that you had just died & so how
could anybody here have that knowledge
but it made me sad in any case to think
about your long & amazing life & the life
of Gwangju people that is so different from
that of the girl walking through Gangnam
wearing a medical mask (not because of flu
but due to a recent visit to the face doctor
& it's not her fault & I don't know anything
about her life but I wonder what's the point
of all this, although I don't expect an answer
from her let alone anyone here I must find my
own reasons for life & carrying on within me

I have to stop thinking about sad things like
the photo of you and Kim Jong-il, hand in
hand at last, while Ko Un looked on; I have
to believe in some sphere of freedom where
girls can walk around wearing short skirts
& holding umbrellas to protect their bleached
faces from harmful gamma rays, & boys
do not have to do their twenty-six
months & old women don't have to live
in basement apartments & crawl up the stairs
& no one tries to steal up-skirt glances at
anyone & tawdry old mats covered with red
peppers spread out to dry can be left in the
middle of the road;

I have to believe in this
road & the reasons for walking alone at night
& so I write & think of you in the past tense
knowing that within hours of your death your
Wikipedia entry had been changed to reflect
the fact & then I knew you were really gone
& it was all beyond dispute, & your life was no
longer an article that doesn't cite its sources
but rather a song free of kidnappers & enemies
& crocodiles crying aloe-vera tears yes forget
that it doesn't matter now, you'll join Roh Moo-hyun
somewhere behind a waterfall & together you'll
wait for the rest of us to arrive (one by one like
days of summer filled with moving tears & hands

& sunshine

Terminal 3: Pan-American Airways

> 'Remember you are free to wander away'
> — John Ashbery, 'As You Came from the Holy Land'

Of course, by the time the assembled heads of state
were seated, the tale of the archaeologist's brushings
was nothing – a melange of WiFi symbols in the air,
because, apparently, 'Here we are, Cofveve, again!'
was not a funny punchline. Your eyes roll in the glare
of entrées limned by dingleberry coulis, tucked away.
Was there ever such a president as this one, present?
And who will be our next? Oh mah Gawd, could it be
the all-too-familiar *Dynasty* theme song? Here, now.
Whatever gloats in the moonlit pits dies, motionless,
like a vortex. The cast sleepwalks through the season
until Joan Collins's arrival: star-spangled, up and blue
and destined, like some smouldering cigarette, to die,
it seems, on every FM station of the cross. A season

you magnanimously declined to categorise accurately,
sitting across from a warlord as you were. Disturbed
as our climate, or sea monkeys making a run for land.
What on earth, he asks, is the true definition of you?
What kinds of enigmas lie in wait at these crossroads?
What rules over rues, lords our lanes, admires avenues?
Where to now (you gesture) if Texas never whispers?
What beets, cornrows, pipelines, backlogs or hedges?
What about the stately accumulation of burning trees?
The questions pile up but your main course rots away

and yes, there'll be time for post mortems tomorrow,
but now our southern borders train their examination
of moonlight on empty arenas. A tricky word, 'befall':
neither past nor present. Hard, perfect. A cold census,
and recounts based on telephone books of odd names.

Remember the corny bride you almost gave gladly away?
As far as she's concerned, you're forever out of place:
the white bow tie on a sunbed-reddened neck. It's late.
The restroom attendant proffers some well-worn adage.
Is it my hand or the prairie air that makes you tremble?
It could have been that the networks had lost interest,
were considering cutting to shots of El Salvador's sky,
but then somebody close lit a pig and slow-roasted it.

Out on the emerald carpet of the strip, a sun emerges,
its scions gripping miniature models of *The Joshua Tree*
taken down like roadrunners or the weary land. Again,
put coins in the jukebox, play all the feels, or else *Rage*.
Knowing you, of course, you'll simply shake it about.
Not a criticism: just a hunch based on plotlines past.
Only time will reveal what it has been doing to itself.
As the long lines queue for maple fentanyl, distributed
in plastic baggies, you wonder: what the actual fuck is
when? And you stumble on the anthems of the past.

Victor Garber Blooper Reel

for alicia sometimes

Victor, I happened to be cruising YouTube recently and
I noticed someone had put together a compilation of

bloopers from the television series *Alias* (or, to be more
specific, *Alias* bloopers featuring you. now, the blooper

reel protocol, as you know, involves hashing your lines
(preferably more than once (plus, ideally, a lot of laughs

from the actors as well as the crew. in your case, Victor,
the bloopers were what we refer to in the industry as 'on

point', meaning they fulfilled the criteria outlined above.
you see, I've watched many blooper reels, mostly on video

tape (or late-night television specials devoted to specific
programmes or actors. after a while, they tend to become

repetitive, don't they? no doubt, given your experience as a
stage actor, you have your own views on all this. You see,

I note a strong perfectionist streak in your onscreen manner
& can't imagine you'd ever be thrilled to have fluffed a line

but when I see you & Sydney (alias Jennifer Garner aka babe
blowing minutes of valuable recording time, thoughts of it

fills me with a simple, homespun joy. one commenter noted:
'oohh seeing him makes me forget everything! great actor &

a great singer as well. He's so hot! I love you Victor! hehe.'
need I go on? perhaps. perhaps draw attention (as if

it were needed, to your magnificent pursed lips, from which
no lie or swear word has had a chance to issue. 'so hot,'

indeed! ('I love him too! wish I had a boyfriend like him XD
sorry, had to write this! :D' ('who cares if he's gay?' & I can't

believe I wrote that ('literally devastated' (Sydney's gay dad.
but back to your pursed lips, Victor. why the heck did you

let the blooper sneak out like that? whenever I rewatch your
blooper reel (which I've added to my 'Favourites' & 'Watch

Later' lists) I begin to doubt your professionalism as an actor.
this sounds harsh, no doubt, but your job (Victor, is to keep

those lips of yours shut tight as a purse, so that no phrase or
object passes in or out (apart from food & drink, of course,

although that must needs happen off camera, in your trailer
or else the on-set canteen (did you go there, Victor, join

the gaffers, grips and gophers at the bain-marie, crack gags as
the caterers wiped down tables? (somehow even the idea

of it sounds far-fetched. you'd be too busy being mesmerised
by Jennifer's bubbly antics, or chatting with the director

in the hopes of slipping in one more tight-lipped rendition of
your daughter's name in a tense ops-room scene (but then

they're all tense when you're onscreen, Victor, which makes
your blooper reel even more alarming (to suggest there is

in fact no real father on which Jack Bristow's character is based
as if Sydney, born an orphan (& this greying Canadian with

a background in musicals was never her uptight/loveable dad
(taken from her, used against her (some other show where

there are no blooper reels, only trailers for the coming season
next: Victor Garber hints at *Alias* reunion.

comments disabled.

(On the tomb of) Yun Hye-yong

Everything you read here is a lie
propagated by diehard fans of
the Pochonbo Electronic Ensemble;

they were a great band, we are told
in an epic poem which you cannot read
because you do not understand music –

I mean, *chuch'e*. The *Chosun Ilbo*
says so, and thus it is foretold; but
everything you read here is a lie. No-

one you know has ever heard of
the Wangjaesan Light Music Band
but that's all right, I'm here to help.

Kim Jong Il loved Yun Hye-yong
but she was dead keen on the guy
who tinkled the ivories for Pochonbo;

which was probably a big mistake
but again I'm just guessing here –
I couldn't say that I liked their music

for sure until I heard it on YouTube
accompanied by a video featuring
pixellated characters from the Sims;

well done, you – whoever you are!
but again, this is beside the point,
which is that Yun Hye-yong fell for

the completely wrong guy, obviously;
and it's tragic and it's cruel to say
but there's no worse way to die

than to throw yourself from the top
of a North Korean banquet hall,
hand in hand with your piano-playing

lover (who dies), only to be 'saved'
by someone acting on the big guy's
orders – yes, and then to be executed

for spurning the big guy's advances;
oh and then to be mythologised in
some other guy's epic poem about

the tragic lovers of Kim Jong Il;
it's not funny – rather, it's plain
to me that somebody had it in for

Yun Hye-yong from the start –
and I'm not talking about the big
guy, who surely had many options;

no, I'm talking about the *Chosun*'s
nationalistic editors, who chose to
run with this trash (for the sake of

truth? musical taste? or something
resembling sensationalism), quoting
the usual North Korean mouthpiece

spouting trash across the sea in Japan,
the kind of junk you'd expect from
the makers of *Team America*, the kind

of stuff we can all laugh at forever;
well, I'm pretty sure Yun Hye-yong
would have preferred to live a little

longer instead, maybe settle down,
start a solo career, sever all ties with
her former band (except the piano

guy, of course, who'd play a minor
role in her life story, and would be
satisfied with that; unlike Mr K, who

we can continue to laugh at, and talk
of orgies at the High Command, his
agents sent to Europe to buy her stuff,

her music the soundtrack to *Arirang*;
but do we know how the story ends,
in a dismal display of mysogynistic

violence, with Yun Hye-yong still in
a coma, the radio playing 'Socialism
is Good', and the keyboards swelling

over a Boney M beat? and while it's
safe to say I still have no clue as to
the veracity of any of these details,

I can almost guarantee nobody will
remember Yun Hye–yong next year –
shot because she loved the wrong guy;

how pathetic is the world, how typical
and true. Yun Hye–yong! Come back!
Tell me everything I read here is a lie.

Terminal 4: Trans-Australia Airlines

> 'As if the argument of trees were done'
> —Kenneth Slessor, 'South Country'

tired of the self-imposed anonymity –
the samizdat, the zines all gone bush –
I feel the twerk of a groomer's brush:
a place I have no right to call Country

my trivial guilts and feels are so done,
performative as phantasmal pains;
I fly in and out on brand-new planes
then preach a carbon-free solution

I am officially over poems about farms
want to see first nations take them back
silence the pub jocks talking down Blak
replace 1980s radio with thunderstorms

oh who's that, there on a shaking ridge?
some outback Fauve with a deck of light?
unmistakable even from this height
(he will never be at home on the beach)

but sure, let's focus on the paddocks bare
a galah's *sotto-voce* shrieks turned pitiful;
some lens flare irradiates an ancient skull
and the voice of hope freezes in mid-air

An cat dubh

o *if they airbrushed my face* could I be a rocket
        or could I somehow perhaps evolve into a star
a sort of rock star cold and dead long abandoned
        somewhere out in space (or else Temple Bar
or maybe Blackpool (UK playing *an cat dubh* with
        a hint of irony in my personal remediation pod
'what noisy cats are we' pipes up Mike (Oldfield
        for some reason, chiming with that inane hankie
dance he always does (but god bless him by gum
        I'm from a band called U2 we're not from Derry
we're from *dubh linn* Blackpool as you say it's
        a dead star the shape and size of a human head
(no prizes for guessing whose & *this is a song about*
        a black cat we may very well have stolen off Charles
Manson who may have even flogged it from The Beatles
        (whom we still haven't actually got around to –
(like, um

                stealing it back?

                                she-kaaaaat

Wireless

The tower was locked (its future being chained to the mast
        like a breeze crossed with water from the past tense (that
immense wall of sound's collage (its anagram eye, loveless
        wireless) abstract but intact. Your childhood lies like party
lines populated by ghosts (some Fenian, others pulled from
        the CSIRO telephone directory. The first email (never sent
CCed Gaia but bounced. *So it goes …* (that manual exchange
        inside a Powerhouse (a museum exhibit etched in charcoal
rides the lightning (killing composers, developing in still-life.
        Meanwhile, father's crystal set gathers dust in a council tip.
The volume & tuning knobs had fallen off anyway, replaced
        by one-cent coins (also obsolescent. A smell it gave when
'live' could trigger memories you never knew you had back
        then, in the *then* when events unfolded in a logical fashion,
proceeding to their happy ending, or a lesson (the Masonic
        Temple's front yard littered with broken glass, dead weeds
(ah that crazy guy who ran screaming down the street (that
        joke about *Oddfellows* isn't so funny now, in his aftermath,
the grey dawn of dead things screwed into the sky (that line
        of furrows from the ground wavered across his forehead, an
object of ridicule allowed one last laugh (surprised to end up
        on someone's thrown-away camera (your soul locked inside
a mangled memory chip (just an SD card away from rapture
        (or was it repatriation? as shards of laughter escaped from
the abandoned Sun Memorial (a sound came out of the blue
        sky *like, as if from nowhere* (a disembodied voice he thought
he'd heard on the antique television set describing Vietnam
        was God (turned out it was the government
                        (calling him up.

His Heart Was an Empty Hotel

He was unknown to me, a phantom bird. Our flight paths intersected momentarily, somewhere over a sandalwood sea. I dreamed of empty hotels in the desert. Stories that never seemed to begin or end. The virus came and I was stranded in an airport, feeling lonely. That much was real. My heart was bruised. Someone said the oil wells were on fire. I laughed and turned to the sporting pages, the latest extinct frog. The coffee grew bitter and cold in its porcelain cup. I drew moons on my breasts in the dark. A sniper drew out my tongue and bit it off. Confiscated it. A thud, inside the theatre. Detonated bombs. Now, I circle the lobby, translating his dim messages into the code I use to breathe. The smoke from the sabotaged pipeline, evidence of cigars in a private club. Plans for my eventual evacuation, on hold. I tuned a radio to their world service, laughed again at the inaccuracy of the reports. Still, in the empty hotel, when I found him, the music screeched. I remembered a dance step from my youth and drew diagrams in chalk on the marble. Commenced my private hopscotch. Incredible, isn't it? In the magazines that arrive daily, always a month ahead of schedule, I see my own words and blanch. That final interview. His strangled noises. Bi-planes and Range Rovers. Sweet whispers. Do not assume that you know me. Who he was, who I became. I shall be my own search party, drenched in sweat, walking down a corridor. His heart was an empty hotel. Mine's still there.

It's Real

It's here and it's real, like snow. Trucks carrying newsprint clog the freeways with its rumour. I was walking along beside it. Something about its timing, its velocity, struck me. I thought, for the first time, that it might be real. It is. It's here, inside this word. It's a breathless world. It's a mountain. Its shadows are cool in summer. Its slopes are the reclined thighs of a human being. It walks beside me in the evening. We have no use for silence any longer. Bottles of it have been brewed from bees. It's there, just like you and me. It's alive and it's real. It's the arcane magic of a long string of digits, or a phone number. It's local. It has a destination. Its timezone is fluid. It breathes. It is the silhouette of a flower. Children know of it. Animals knew of it, once. Its cogs and wheels whirr. They know of it. I could see it in the moon. Winter knows its warmth. Stars do not. Sailors sing to it. Birds do not have wings. I do not even dare to breathe. It lingers, in the frost. It's here and it's real, like rain.

More sun than clouds; sprinkles early

said let's buy tulips because you were homesick
twenty-four hour florists late-night emergencies

the tulips sat inside a cool store freezer still wet
& trembling fragile as a whispered wish (we said

let's buy some tulips today there's more sun than
cloud their powers are quite expensive but what

does money matter (when there's more sun than
clouds scanning the supermarket aisles for some

sprinkles early in the morning (we said let's buy
some sprinkles when you were thinking of home

I was thinking of the sun we took photographs of
tulips they were orange as bushfire suns (& wet

as clouds & our faces looking up to see sprinkles
saw twinkles in the blank sky (homesick & here

The Day Britney Died

I was standing in the bathroom shaving my head
when the news came through & I just, you know,

choked up: I must have had a kind of emotional
malfunction because I kept scratching my face,

like it was a stranger's. Stunned by the shrill levity
that followed, all the drive-time scrambling for

moronic puns. As far as I could tell no one really
cared about Britney at all. It was as if she hadn't

actually died, only gone crazy, maybe shaved her
head for cancer research. As I looked at the tufts

of my hair on the tiles I started crying but I didn't
know why. For some reason they reminded me

of French collaborators during the war, women
paraded in village squares & their shaved heads.

The self-righteous stares & the grim satisfaction:
as if you could eradicate someone's shame with

a pair of clippers & therefore exonerate society (or
just yourself. I swept up my dwindling clumps

& thought – it's no use selling this on Ebay, is it?
when it just grows back (unlike a severed head.

I switched off the radio & Britney was still dead.

Sparrow dabang

for Terry Jaensch

Last night I heard Yi Sang sing in a *noraebang*
sounding just like a little sparrow does going
tang tang tacka tacka tk tk tk tk tang, it was
such a sad little song that sparrow sang
the kind that nobody else knew the words to
but don't think that stopped him – no way!
I can hear Yi Sang still, on the hanok roof
going *tang tang tacka tacka tk tk tk tk tang*

all day long, in dead silence, like a sparrow.

Then I saw Yi Sang playing Starcraft in a PC *bang*
losing badly, screaming at the screen, the air
heavy with teenage smoke and his keyboard
sticky from grape soda (do you think that stopped
Yi Sang? never! losing men and energy way too
fast to ever keep up with his competitors going
tang tang tacka tacka tk tk tk tk tang on
their worn-out keyboards all night long,

in networked silence, like a flock of sparrows.

Then (if you can believe this) I saw Yi Sang
soaking himself in a *jjimjilbang*, his hair like
feathers on the head of a sparrow, spiky and
wet, like a sparrow drinking from the smallest
puddle you can imagine. as if wet feathers could

ever hold him back, don't believe it! Yi Sang, wet,
sitting in a pool in a *jjimjilbang* for hours on end,
his little heart racing as if he was flying through

air going *tang tang tacka tacka tk tk tk tk tang.*

Tonight I'm sitting quietly in a corner of a *dabang*
thinking of Yi Sang and what he would have made
of the new *multibang* craze. maybe he would have
liked it, maybe there's a place for a little sparrow
inside a pay-as-you-go *multitang*, a little space
that goes *tang tang tacka tacka tk tk tk tk tang*
all day long if you want, if that's what you want,
if that's what makes you happy. don't you think

it's a nice idea? a nice way to re-imagine Yi Sang?

& tomorrow I'll be sitting in a DVD *bang*, watching
a movie based on the life of Yi Sang. I won't see
a single sparrow, I won't even hear the sound
a sparrow makes in a tree in the dark. don't you
know? don't you believe in the sound a sparrow
makes in the dark? never mind, I can remind you,
it sounds like *tang tang tacka tacka tk tk tk tk tang*,
all night long, in a corner of a sparrow *dabang*,

like the most beautiful, lonely sound in the world.

Three Rings

—Grizzly Bear

in less than five minutes from now you will appear
like a shuddering ruin or the crypto-melodic outro
that's shaking me awake for absolutely no reason –

don't you ever leave me! I scream while all your spiders
scuttle away into their reaches of pencil-drawn web
there's Frankie, you note, perched calmly on the rim

go well wherever you are, fly into the terrestrial sun
leave many letters behind on crumpled bits of paper
I will gather them all & put them straight in the bin

here, take this hammer from me and make its song
implode just like a battle scene only now in reverse
then activate the airlock (as the endless night rings

I will push our dreams like stars out into the snow
zip you into your brand-new all-purpose bodysuit
other people can struggle with the science for once

The Day Heath Ledger Died

well, on the day Heath Ledger died I was watching *Sunrise* –
surrounded by pills they said first he's dead & then the ads

& then in breaking news, this: so, Jo, what does it *mean*?
cut to Wednesday's expert from '*New Ikea*' magazine (who

brings H. Ledger back to life no suggestion of suicide & yet
troubled Hollywood fame & divorce his children the strain

seething on red media carpets uncomfortable with the game
Brokeback Mountain of course nominated for an Oscar there

but we're back in the present-tense NBC press conference:
surrounded by pills says Kochie dead at twenty-eight in sad

in shocking breaking news Heath Ledger found dead in NYC
at twenty-eight (surrounded by pills for fuck's sake (Ledger

barely hours dead & *this* already? dead on *Sunrise* if you've
just joined us surrounded by pills Heath Ledger our thoughts

our condolences to his family it appears surrounded by pills
okay you're watching *Sunrise* on the day Heath Ledger died)

Kus

& if I ever learn a word of Dutch –
        as in really learn it know its body
then the only word I want to know is
        kus: this beautiful word for a kiss
or is it to kiss as in the verb to be
        to be a stranger in the mouth of
another language another way of
        breathing after all isn't that just
another way of writing language
        the way the mind breathes air &
creates tangible concepts like to
        be as in I am or we are they're not

& then to move on to know plurals
        as in *kussen* the verb couple to be
a pair of kisses against my lips as
        in the curve of this chocolate egg
to know space between two kisses
        & to understand the possibility of
breathing meaning into chocolate
        chickens or word lovers in Dutch
after all there are several points at
        which our languages rest against
each other like two tired bicyclists
        kissing forever in a quiet lane

& to know the space of this space
        the physical meaning of a word not
meant to live in a dictionary but in
        the mouth to move through Dutch
like stars through unexplored space
        after all isn't language like a shiny
spaceship forever tumbling towards
        the *kus* the *kussen* the be the to be
bright & exploding stars our lives
        full of curved static words we wish
to move between like stations on
        space lines our destination *kussen*

& if I ever learn the word for *kus*
        in my own half-language in which
I could have been born to be to not
        be heard to speak without hearing
the smack of that *kus* against the
        porthole spaces to hear it coming
or departing perhaps upon arrival
        I will breathe in that kiss-filled air
& know its velocity its private *kus*
        in between *kussen* as soft shadows
born of lips parse what is felt into
        being to be I am to kiss to be alive

ACKNOWLEDGEMENTS

Various journals have accepted the poems in this collection for publication, either in print or online. My thanks to the editors and publishers of *Best of Australian Poems 2024*, *continent.*, *Cordite Poetry Review*, *Ekleksographia*, *FourW*, *Jacket2*, OCHO, *Overland*, *Page 17*, *Peril*, *The Red Room* and *Shipwrights Review*.

Special thanks to Ivy Alvarez, Emilie Zoey Baker, Pam Brown, Michael Farrell, Johanna Featherstone, Liam Ferney, Terry Jaensch, Jill Jones, Klare Lanson, Bronwyn Lay, Jooyoung Lee, Kate Lilley, Nic Lowe, Kent MacCarter, Greg McLaren, Trisha Pender, Felicity Plunkett, Boel Schenlaer, Alicia Sometimes, Victoria Stanton, Sean M Whelan, Adrian Wiggins and Ed Wright.

Earlier versions of some of these poems originally appeared in self-published chapbooks. Others were posted online at daveydreamnation.com or sent to subscribers to my 'Poem of the Week' newsletter.

'Kus' received the 2007 June Shenfield Poetry Award (with the title 'space kus'), and was later translated into Macedonian for the *Struga Poetry Evenings Anthology* (2011). 'Т’га за југ' is a free transliteration of Graham W Reid's translation of 'T'ga za jug' [Longing for the South] by Konstantin Miladinov (1830–62). 'come with me, through' first appeared in a chapbook issued by Sydney Poetry in 2010 as part of its First Friday readings series. My thanks to Adrian Wiggins for producing it.

'clouds, afternoon, jazz, sprinkles' first appeared online as part of the Red Room Company's 'The Disappearing' Project in 2012. The quotes in 'Victor Garber Blooper Reel' are all user comments posted in response to *Alias* compilations on YouTube.

The terminal form popularised by John Tranter (1943–2023) uses the end word on each line of a poem to create a new work. Three of the four terminals in this collection take a slightly different approach, using both the start *and* end words on each line of the source poem.

Some poems in this collection were written during an Asialink residency in Seoul, Republic of Korea, in 2009. My thanks to the Asialink Centre at the University of Melbourne and the Literature Translation Institute of Korea.

David Prater was born in Dubbo in 1972. He spent his childhood in various country towns before moving to Sydney to study Australian literature in the early 1990s. Over the past four decades, his poetry has been published in a range of Australian and international journals and anthologies. Papertiger Media published his first full-length poetry collection, *We Will Disappear*, in 2007. Puncher and Wattmann published his second, *Leaves of Glass*, in 2014. Between 2001 and 2012, he was Managing Editor of *Cordite Poetry Review*. He has worked as a writer, researcher and editor in a number of educational, intergovernmental and academic settings. He currently lives with his spouse and three children in a small village in Fryslân, the Netherlands.